Along the Seashore

Rod Theodorou

Heinemann Library
Chicago, Illinois

Designed by AMR
Illustrations by Art Construction and Darrell Warner at Beehive Illustration
Printed by Wing King Tong, in Hong Kong

04 03 02 01
10 9 8 7 6 5 4 3 2

Library of Congress Cataloging-in-Publication Data
Theodorou, Rod.
      Along the seashore / Rod Theodorou.
          p. cm. -- (Amazing journeys)
      Includes bibliographical references.
      Summary: Explores the geology and life fors of seashores,
including cliffs, sand dunes, the splash zone, low-tide area,
shallows, and deep water, discussing their plants and animals,
environmental challenges, and conservation efforts.
      ISBN 1-57572-483-9 (library binding)
      1. Seashore biology Juvenile literature. 2. Seashore Juvenile
literature.   [1. Seashore biology 2. Seashore.} I. Title.
II. Series: Telford, Carole, 1961–   Amazing journeys.
QH95.7.T54 2000
578.769'9--dc21   99-37161
                                                    CIP

Acknowledgments

The Publishers would like to thank the following for permission to reproduce photographs:

Bruce Coleman/Dr Eckart Pott, p. 14; Bruce Coleman/Jan Van de Kam, p. 10; FLPA/M. B. Withers, p. 6; Oxford Scientific
Films/Andrew Plimptre, p. 13; Oxford Scientific Films/Barrie Watts, p. 15, Oxford Scientific Films/Colin Milkins, p. 25, Oxford
Scientific Films/David Cayless, p. 27; Oxford Scientific Films/David Fleetham, p.19; Oxford Scientific Films/David Thompson, pp.
16, 17; Oxford Scientific Films/G. I. Bernard, pp. 15, 21, 23; Oxford Scientific Films/Howard Hall, p. 23; Oxford Scientific
Films/London Scientific Films, p. 13; Oxford Scientific Films/Mark Hambin, p. 11; Oxford Scientific Films/Michael Leach, p. 11;
Oxford Scientific Films/Mike Hill, p. 26; Oxford Scientific Films/Paul Kay, pp. 19, 25; Oxford Scientific Films/Raj Kamal, p. 7;
Oxford Scientific Films/Stan Osolinski, p. 21; Oxford Scientific Films/Zig Leszczynski, p. 24.

Cover photograph reproduced with permission of Planet Earth Pictures.

Every effort has been made to contact copyright holders of any material reproduced in this book. Any omissions will be rectified
in subsequent printings if notice is given to the Publisher.

Some words are shown in bold, **like this.**
You can find out what they mean by looking in the glossary

Contents

Introduction

You are about to go on an amazing journey. You are going to travel across a rocky north–Atlantic coast beach and down into the ocean waves. This is a harsh and dangerous world, a battleground between the sea and the land. It is called the seashore or shoreline.

All **continents** have a shoreline. North America alone has over 96,000 miles (160,000 kilometers) of shoreline. As the waves crash against shoreline cliffs, they break away pieces of rock. These are rolled by the waves on the seabed until they become smooth pebbles. After hundreds of years, the pebbles wear away to tiny grains of sand. On some shallow parts of the coast, waves carry this sand onto the land and form beaches. We are going to travel across a beach.

All parts of a shoreline are different. Some parts have no beach at all—tall cliffs of rock rise straight out of the sea.

Living things have a hard time surviving on seashores, mainly because of the **tides**. As our moon circles Earth, it pulls on Earth's seas. This pull causes the **sea level** to rise higher and then fall lower, changing each day and each month, depending on where the moon is. This means the waves do not always stop at the same place on the shore. Sometimes they end at the bottom of the beach. This is low tide. Sometimes they rise right up and flood the top of the beach. This is high tide.

Plants and animals that live on the seashore have to be able to survive the effects of both waves and tides. Sometimes they are covered in foaming cold waves, and at other times they are left to dry out and bake in the hot sun. What plants and animals could live in this ever-changing world of hot rock and cold water?

At low tide on a beach, we can see the seaweed that usually lives under the water.

Journey Map

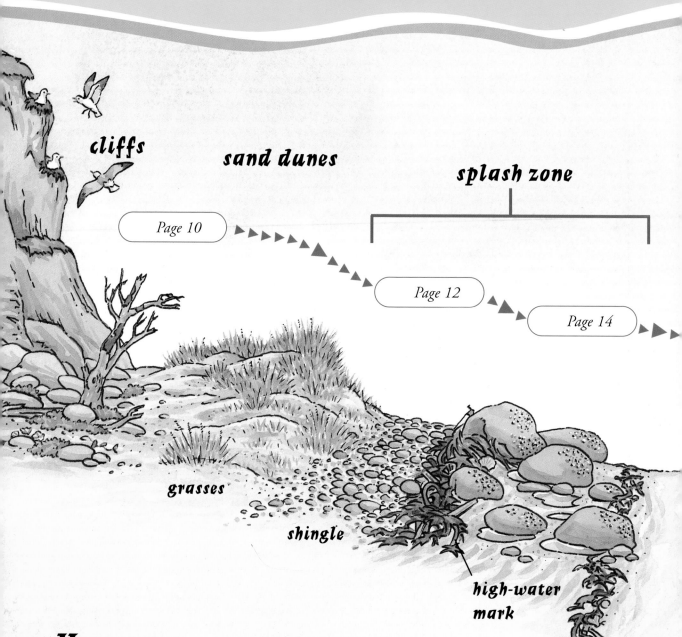

cliffs

sand dunes

splash zone

Page 10

Page 12

Page 14

grasses

shingle

high-water
mark

strandline

Here is a map of our journey. Each part of the seashore is different. We begin our journey at the foot of the cliffs and walk through grassy sand dunes. No water ever reaches this far up the beach, except in very violent storms. The **strandline** and high-water mark show the highest point the waves reach at high **tide**.

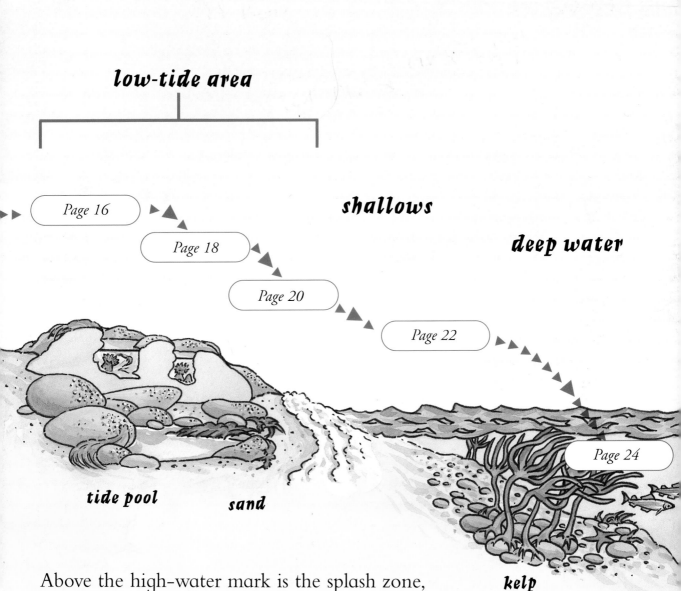

low-tide area

Page 16

Page 18

shallows

Page 20

deep water

Page 22

Page 24

tide pool

sand

kelp

Above the high-water mark is the splash zone, a hostile world of baking rock and cold spray. Every tide leaves a strandline, a "graveyard" for dead animals and seaweed carried by the water. We travel down the beach and into the waves.

Cliffs and Dunes

We are standing at the foot of huge cliffs. We can see seabirds flying overhead. Many of them come to the cliffs to lay eggs on the tiny ledges. We walk among the large stones and boulders to the sand dunes. The wind blows dry sand across the dunes, stinging against our legs. We can taste tiny droplets of salt water carried by the wind. The sun beats down on our necks. There is no shelter here and not much life. Only tough little plants, such as thyme and lavender, can survive this dry, salty desert. They are low-growing to avoid the wind, and they have tough, thick leaves that store water.

One of the most important plants here is marram grass. It helps form the sand dunes that give a little shelter for other plants and some nesting birds, such as this tern.

Kittiwakes

Like many seabirds, kittiwakes nest on cliff edges where they are safe from **predators** and yet near to the sea where they can catch fish.

Marram grass

Marram grass has very deep roots that can spread up to 30 feet (9 meters) a year. Its roots hold sand in place, keeping it from blowing away. Marram grass can form high dunes.

Sand dunes

A simple piece of dead seaweed can start a huge sand dune! **1)** As the seaweed rots, wind blows sand around it. **2)** If a piece of marram grass takes root there, it holds the tiny sand dune in place. **3)** If the weather is calm, the grass will grow, and a large dune may form.

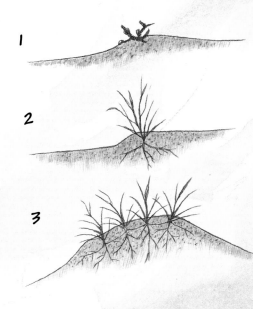

At the Strandline

We walk carefully on a sand-dune path down onto the shingle. Shingle is made from millions of small pebbles and pieces of shell. Crunching our way across the shingle, we reach a line of dead seaweed stretching across the beach. This is a strandline, which shows how high the water has come during a **tide.** Flies buzz around and there is a strong smell of rotting seaweed. Lying among the seaweed is an amazing collection of things dumped here by the high tide. We can see dead fish and crabs, broken seashells, driftwood, plastic bags, and a child's plastic shovel. These are all clues to the life that can be found on the beach and beneath the waves.

1. limpet
2. mussel
3. barnacle
4. oyster
5. dog whelk
6. razor clam
7. winkle
8. top shell
9. scallop
10. kelp
11. cuttlefish bone
12. bladder wrack
13. mermaid's purse
14. sea urchin skeleton

Many people enjoy **beachcombing**, which means looking for shells and other interesting things along the beach.

Bladder wrack

This seaweed has pouches of air growing in its branches. They keep the huge seaweed upright underwater. Storms often rip up bladder wrack and dump it on the beach.

Sand hoppers

If you lift up dead seaweed, you may see thousands of tiny creatures hopping around. These sand hoppers, or beach fleas, live under rocks and seaweed and are often eaten by shorebirds.

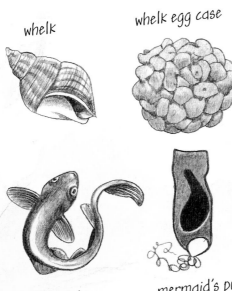

whelk

whelk egg case

dogfish

mermaid's purse

Empty egg cases

Whelks are sea snails that lay bundles of eggs fixed to stones underwater. The empty cases are often washed onto beaches. Mermaid's purses are the empty egg cases of dogfish, a kind of shark.

The Splash Zone

Above each strandline is an area reached only by splashes from waves. It is cooler in a splash zone, but it is still a very difficult place to live. When the waves do not splash, this area is hot and dry. At other times, the wind blows sea spray up here, making it very salty. When high **tide** does reach this high, it covers everything in cold seawater. When it is stormy, the waves may toss sand and stones against the rocks. Only very tough little animals can survive in the splash zone. Living on the salty rocks are **lichens**, a few small sea snails, and thousands of limpets and barnacles.

Thousands of barnacles grow in a belt along the splash zone of many shorelines.

Barnacles

These animals have very tough shells that are stuck onto the rocks like concrete. When covered with water, the tops of the shells open and the animals catch tiny pieces of food with their feathery **tentacles.**

Dog whelk

This is a meat-eating snail that attacks and eats barnacles. It has a small **spine** that it uses to open up a barnacle's shell.

Limpets

Each limpet has a strong sucker foot that clamps it tightly onto a rock. If another limpet comes too close to it, it pushes its shell under the other limpet's until the intruder moves away.

Into a Tide Pool

The region between high tide and low tide is the intertidal zone. Life is difficult here because living conditions change constantly. Sometimes rocks in the intertidal zone trap pools of seawater. These tide pools are home to many shoreline animals. The animals that live here in the tide pool's cool, dark depths are safe from the hot sun and pounding waves. Every day, waves wash into the pool, bringing new seawater and food. Tide pools can also be very tough places to live. When it rains, the pool may fill up with **fresh water**. When the sun shines, some water dries up, making what is left hot and salty. Seagulls may come and peck at the animals in the pool, trying to eat them.

Some tide pools are filled with new seawater every day. Others may go for days before the tide is high enough to reach them.

Mussels

Thousands of these smooth black **shellfish** grow on rocks across most shorelines. They have tough threads growing out of their base that grip onto the rock.

Anemones

Out of the water, an anemone looks like a dull blob of jelly stuck on a rock. When the water level reaches it, the anemone spreads its colorful arms. Each of these **tentacles** can sting and catch small **prey**.

Shore crabs

These tough crabs are like little tanks. They feed on shellfish, which they crack open with their strong claws. Be careful if you pick one up – even the smallest crabs can give a painful pinch!

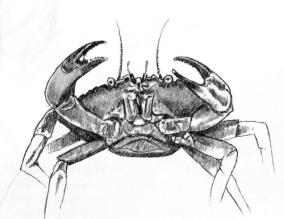

A Tiny Sea

Every **tide** pool is a tiny, amazing world. Beautiful shrimp swim through the colorful gardens of seaweed and anemones. Some shrimp are **transparent**, making them very hard for **predators** to spot. Tiny fish dart from one hiding place to another, always on the lookout for danger. They hide under stones or in rocky **crevices**. Crabs scuttle along the bottom of the pool snatching up scraps of food. Some animals live all their lives in the tide pool. Others, such as the large **edible** crab, are trapped by the tides and will escape as soon as the waves return.

1. limpet
2. mussel
3. wrack
4. periwinkle
5. winkle
6. blenny
7. goby
8. anemone
9. velvet swimming crab
10. shrimp
11. cushion star
12. hermit crab
13. edible crab

Tide pools are wonderful places to look for seashore life, but do not take any of the creatures away.

Hermit crab

These tiny crabs have no shell of their own. They live in the shells of dead sea snails. When they grow too big for one shell, they quickly crawl out and hop into a bigger new shell.

Goby

This tiny fish has a sucker on its belly to help it grip the rocks when the waves wash into the pool. It has bulging eyes on the top of its head to look upward for seagulls and other predators.

Shrimp

Shrimp walk or swim slowly forward around the pool. If attacked, they pull their tails back suddenly. This movement shoots them backward, away from danger.

On the Beach

We are now moving down the slope of the beach toward the waves. It is cooler and very fresh here. The waves wash up the beach, wetting the sand. We cannot see any animals at all and yet there are thousands all around us—right beneath our feet!

A huge number of worms, sea snails, starfish, and other small animals live buried in the wet sand. Some scrape tiny pieces of food off the sand itself. Others are hiding from **predators**, waiting for the **tide** to rise. When it does, this part of the beach will be underwater for a few hours. The hidden animals come out of their burrows and feed off tiny **particles** of food in the seawater.

1. oystercatcher
2. lugworm
3. cockle
4. razor shell
5. burrowing starfish
6. sea potato
7. sea mouse

Shorebirds, such as sanderlings and oystercatchers, run up and down the beach hunting for hidden **shellfish** and worms.

Oystercatcher

These shorebirds look for shellfish that poke from the sand with their shells slightly open. The oystercatcher stabs the **muscle** that closes the shell. The bird then opens the shell and eats what is inside.

Lugworm

Thousands of lugworms live in U-shaped burrows under the sand. They leave a little mound of sand, called a **cast**, at the top of their burrow.

Razor shell

The razor shell is named after old-fashioned razors. It burrows into the sand with its muscular foot. Its thin shape helps it slide down its burrow if attacked by a predator.

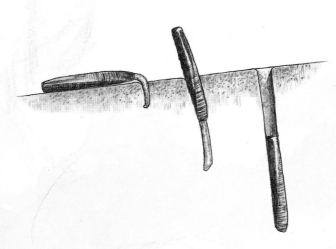

Kelp Forests

We put on our **masks** and **snorkels** and wade into the chilly water. Small waves slap against us. We take a deep breath and dive into the shallows.

All around us are long, brown, underwater weeds growing from the seabed up toward the light. The weeds wave backward and forward as the waves roll in above. This long seaweed is called kelp. Each kelp plant has rootlike organs called **holdfasts,** which grip onto the rocks and seabed. Kelp covers the seabed in a long strip, just like a forest. This forest is important as a home for many animals. Sea urchins and limpets graze on the kelp. Fish, crabs, and starfish are kelp forest **predators,** moving through the holdfasts looking for food.

Kelp forests protect many animals from the heat of the sun and the force of the waves.

Kelp

Kelp grows only in water about 10 feet (3 meters) deep, where there is still plenty of sunlight. Giant kelp grows in warm, bright water that is much deeper. Giant kelp can reach lengths of up to 100 feet (30 meters) and can grow a yard (almost 1 meter) in just one day!

Sea urchin

Sea urchins have tough, sharp jaws under their ball-shaped bodies. They move slowly through the kelp, feeding on its **stipes** and holdfasts. Sharp **spines** protect the urchins from predators.

Dogfish

A dogfish is a small kind of shark that lays its eggs among kelp. The egg cases have **tendrils** at the ends that wind around the stalk to hold the egg in place (see page 13).

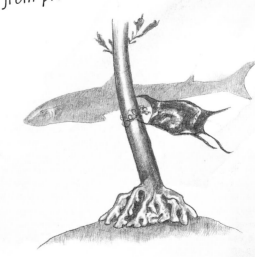

Beyond the Shallows

We swim out of the dark, dense kelp forest into deeper water. There is a long stretch of flat sand on the seabed beneath us. We swim down to the sand and glide just above it. We cannot see any signs of life. Suddenly there is a burst of sand in front of us and we see something swim away. We have disturbed a large flatfish, which was almost invisible against the sand. There are many other creatures hidden here under the sand or among the clumps of rocks and weed.

The sun is going down, and the water is getting cold. Many more creatures will come out at night to feed. It is time to end our journey and return to the shore.

Lobsters live in deeper waters, hiding in holes among the rocks. They come out at night to look for dead fish and other scraps of food.

Turbot

This flatfish can change the color of its skin to match the color of the sand and rocks around it. In this way, the flatfish stays hidden from **predators** and can gobble up smaller fish that come too close.

Acorn barnacle

Barnacles live on rocks in huge numbers. Sometimes it is hard to find any space left on a rock. Here, acorn barnacles have found a quite different home—on top of a mussel shell!

Piddock

A piddock is a relative of mussels and clams. The end of a piddock looks like an oil drill **bit**. Just like a drill, it turns around and around to grind its way through sand, or even rock, to make a **burrow**.

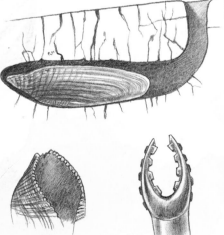

end of piddock shell   oil drill bit

Conservation and the Future

The seashore is a wonderful place to visit, but it is also an easy place to damage. Cliff edges and sand dunes are important as homes to nesting seabirds. Too many tourists scare the birds away and may **erode** the cliff edges. Sand dunes are also easily damaged by people. If a person pulls up a chunk of marram grass, the wind can whistle through the hole left in the sand dune. Soon the hole gets wider and wider until it destroys the dune. Walking over rocks can also crush and kill barnacles and other **shellfish**.

Pollution is a much bigger threat. Chemicals and sewage dumped into the water kill fish, seaweed, and shellfish. Oil spills can kill thousands of seabirds and ruin beaches for hundreds of miles.

The seashores of the northeastern United States and the Mediterranean Sea have been badly polluted in the past.

Protecting the seashore

Many countries are now trying to look after their seashores and coastlines. They have stopped sewage dumping near the shore and cleaned oil off their beaches. Some have turned hundreds of miles of coastline into national parks where the wildlife is protected from pollution.

You can help protect the seashore. Always use paths and walkways that have been built through sand dunes. Do not take anything alive away from the seashore or a tide pool. If you turn over a rock to look underneath, put it back carefully. Never leave garbage on the beach. Unless we protect these wonderful places, there will be no more amazing journeys to make along the seashore.

These people are clearing up oil that has spilled on a beach.

Glossary

beachcombing	collecting things that have washed up onto the beach
bit	cutting part of a drill
burrow	hole an animal makes in the sand or ground to use for shelter
cast	sand pushed up on the surface where a worm has tunneled down into the beach
continent	one of the seven large areas of land that make up the world
crevice	narrow crack
edible	good or safe to eat
erode	to wear away
freshwater	fresh river or stream water, not salty seawater
holdfast	rootlike structure on some plants that grip a surface to hold the plant in place
intertidal	between high tide and low tide
lichen	primitive plant that grows on rocks or trees
particle	very small amount of something
pollution	anything that makes air, water, or soil dirty, such as chemicals or trash
predator	animal that hunts, kills, and eats other animals
prey	animals that are hunted by predators
sea level	the height of the sea at different times
shellfish	animal that lives in water and has a hard outer shell, such as an oyster or a mussel

snorkel	tube used by a swimmer swimming just under the surface to get air to breathe
spine	special stiff or pointed fish fin
stipe	stalk of the kelp seaweed
tendril	special leaf or stem that some animals or climbing plants use to fasten themselves to something
tentacle	long and flexible part of some animals that is used to feel or touch
tide	rise and fall of the surface of the sea at different times in response to the pull of the moon
transparent	clear enough to see through

More Books to Read

Armentrout, Patricia. *Waves and Tides.* Vero Beach, Fla.: Rourke Press, 1996.

Crump, Donald. *The World's Wild Shores.* Washington, D.C.: National Geographic Society, 1990.

Gallant, Roy. *Sand on the Move: The Story of Dunes.* Danbury, Conn.: Franklin Watts, 1997.

Hartley, Linda. *Hermit Crab Moves House.* Ada, Okla.: Garrett Educational Corporation, 1996.

Massa, Renato. *Along the Coasts.* Austin, Tex.: Raintree Steck-Vaughn, 1998.

Paul, Tessa. *By the Seashore.* New York: Crabtree Publishing Co., 1997.

Perry, Phyllis J. *Sea Stars and Dragons.* Danbury, Conn.: Franklin Watts, 1996.

Theodorou, Rod, and Carole Telford. *Inside a Coral Reef.* Des Plaines, Ill.:Heinemann Library, 1997.

Theodorou, Rod. *To the Depths of the Ocean.* Chicago: Heinemann Library, 2000.

Organizations

Cousteau Society
870 Greenbrier Circle
Suite 402
Chesapeake, Va. 23320
Tel. (800) 441-4395

Earthwatch Institute U.S.
680 Mount Auburn Street
Watertown, Mass. 02471
Tel. (800) 776-0188

Greenpeace U.S.A.
1436 U Street N.W
Washington, D.C. 20009
Tel. (202) 462-1177

National Wildlife Federation
8925 Leesburg Pike
Vienna, Va. 22184
Tel. (703) 790-4100

Save the Whales
PO Box 2397
Venice, CA 90291

Index